Essensuals, Next Generation Toni & Guy:

Step By Step

Hairdressing And Beauty Industry Authority series – related titles

Hairdressing

Mahogany Hairdressing: Steps to Cutting, Colouring and Finishing Hair by Martin Gannon and Richard Thompson
Mahogany Hairdressing: Advanced Looks by Martin Gannon and Richard Thompson (*publishing October 2001*)
Patrick Cameron: Dressing Long Hair by Patrick Cameron and Jacki Wadeson
Patrick Cameron: Dressing Long Hair Book 2 by Patrick Cameron
Bridal Hair by Pat Dixon and Jacki Wadeson
Trevor Sorbie: Visions in Hair by Kris Sorbie and Jacki Wadeson
The Total Look: The Style Guide for Hair and Make-Up Professionals by Ian Mistlin
Art of Hair Colouring by David Adams and Jacki Wadeson

Start Hairdressing: The Official Guide to Level 1 by Martin Green and Leo Palladino
Hairdressing – The Foundations: The Official Guide to Level 2 by Leo Palladino
Professional Hairdressing: The Official Guide to Level 3 by Martin Green, Lesley Kimber and Leo Palladino
Men's Hairdressing: Traditional and Modern Barbering by Maurice Lister
African-Caribbean Hairdressing by Sandra Gittens
The World of Hair: A Scientific Companion by Dr John Gray
Salon Management by Martin Green

Beauty Therapy

Beauty Therapy – The Foundations: The Official Guide to Level 2 by Lorraine Nordmann
Professional Beauty Therapy: The Official Guide to Level 3 by Lorraine Nordmann, Lorraine Appleyard and Pamela Linforth
Aromatherapy for the Beauty Therapist by Valerie Ann Worwood
The World of Skin Care: A Scientific Companion by Dr John Gray
Indian Head Massage by Muriel Burnham-Airey and Adele O'Keefe
The Complete Nail Technician by Marian Newman
Safety in the Salon by Elaine Almond

Essensuals, Next Generation Toni & Guy:
Step By Step

hair by sacha and christian mascolo

images stuart weston

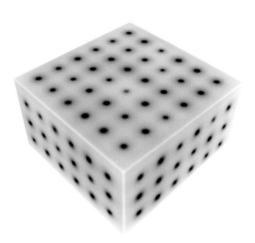

WELLA

HABIA
Hairdressing And Beauty Industry Authority

essensuals
HAIRDRESSING

THOMSON
LEARNING

Australia · Canada · Mexico · Singapore · Spain · United Kingdom · United States

Essensuals, Next Generation Toni & Guy: Step-By-Step

Copyright © Essensuals Group (Sacha Mascolo and Christian Mascolo) and Stuart Weston 2002

The Thomson Learning logo is a registered trademark used herein under licence.

For more information, contact Thomson Learning, Berkshire House, 168–173 High Holborn, London, WC1V 7AA or visit us on the World Wide Web at: http://www.thomsonlearning.co.uk

British Library Cataloguing-in-Publication Data
A catalogue record for this book is available from the British Library

ISBN 1-86152-955-4

Printed in Singapore by Seng Lee

contents

acknowledgements

Creative director: Sacha Mascolo
Educational director: Christian Mascolo

Photography and images by: Stuart Weston
Step-by-step photographer: Collin Ellis
Original design by: Anita Wright
Styled by: Faye Sawyer

Stylist assisted by: Julie Ann Kahl
Photographers assisted by: Vahakn Vorperian (First assistant), Jane Caffrey,
Julia Mckay and Damian Duncan

Hair Step by Step: Sacha Mascolo, Christian Mascolo, Mark Mackelvie,
Lainie Reeves, Ian Daburn, Drew Foster

Technical Step by Steps: Julie Gurr, June Graham, Yumi Dingle, Justin Smith,
Jackie Grier, Kate Williams

Contributors: Amanda Agar
Many thanks to everyone that helped

Makeup: Ginni Bogado, Lucia Pica, Aida De Roo, Talitha Wassel

Translations: Syliva Esparaza, Nina Beckert, Claudia Corbelli
Edited by: Olivia Abbott

Furniture designed by: Ansel Thompson

Models: Antea Schromek, Gabriella Stonebridge, Katie Power, Francesca Knowles, Irene, Iesha, Jamie,
Holly, Ania, Tamanisha, Elka Mocker, Meg Peterson, Helen Stinton, Sorcha, Leona

PR: Alex Walmsley
General Manager: Sue Haydon

preface

This exciting new book contains 20 cutting-edge styles by Essensuals, the "diffusion" line of the Toni & Guy salon group. Illustrated in step-by-step detail with stunning photographic sequences and accompanied by clear instructions in five different languages, this book recreates Essensuals' cutting, technical, afro and make-up techniques and will provide inspiration and instruction for hairdressing professionals. A gallery of images from Essensuals' latest *Interactive Collection* provides further inspiration for both stylists and clients.

The brainchild of Toni Mascolo, co-founder of Toni & Guy, Essensuals was formed in 1997 and has already grown to become an international chain with salons spanning three continents. Toni set up Essensuals with his daughter Sacha – creative director, his son Christian – head of education, and his brother Anthony (three times British Hairdresser of the Year) with the aim of creating a new generation of hairdressing for the 21st century.

Sacha Mascolo has been in the business for 13 years and has a list of clients that reads like a who's who. She is the youngest person to have ever won "Best Newcomer" (in 1990) and won "London Hairdresser of the Year 1999/2000". Christian created the education programme for Essensuals and his expertise and enthusiasm ensures quality styling and technical work is maintained throughout the group. Stuart Weston has collaborated with Essensuals on a number of projects including the winning shots for "London Hairdresser of the Year 1999/2000".

"Anybody who's anybody wants a piece of Essensuals"

Toni Mascolo

antea

Sacha Mascolo
step-by-step cutting
Kate Williams
step-by-step colour

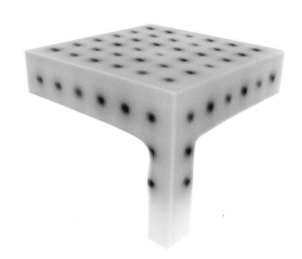

3 Use the back section as a guide and follow it through to the sides taking vertical sections.

3 Utiliser la section postérieure comme guide et continuer sur les côtés de la tête, toujours en prenant des sections verticales.

3 Die hibntereAbteilung wird als Füuhurngslinie benutzt und zu den seiten vertikal bearbeitet.

3 Utilizar la sección de atrás como guia y seguirla hacia los lados tomando secciones verticales.

3 La sezione posteriore viene usata come guida e si continua lungo i lati della testa, sempre prendendo sezioni verticali.

1 The profile section is taken from crown to nape area.

1 Tracer la Section Profil (section centrale des cheveux) en partant du point d'eclatement jusqu'a la nuque.

1 Profillinies wird abgeteilt von wirbel zum Nacken.

1 Tomamos una patición de perfil, que es una sección llevada desde la coronilla hasta la zona de la nuca.

1 Si prende la Sezione Profilo (sezione centrale dei capelli) partendo dalla calotta fino alla nuca.

10

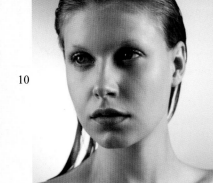  
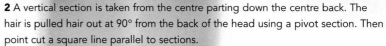 

2 A vertical section is taken from the centre parting down the centre back. The hair is pulled hair out at 90° from the back of the head using a pivot section. Then point cut a square line parallel to sections.

2 Prende une section verticle en partant de la raie centrale en decendant vers la bas, dans la partie centrale postrerieure de la tete. Lisser les cheveux á 90 degrés á l'arrière de la tête ense servant

2 Das Haar wird in 90° winkel vertikal abgelhoben wobei die Abteilungen point-cut geschnitten werden. Der witbel dient hier als mittelpunkt.

2 Sección vertical del centro de la patición hacia la parte baja. Proyectar el cabello a 90° de la. Zona de atrás de la cabeza utilizando una seccion radial y cortar una linea recta a punta de tijera paralela a la sección.

2 Si prende una sez verticale dal centro della test fino ad arrivare all'orecchio. Poi portando I capelli all'infuori all'infuori al retro della testa usando I 90 ed "point cutting".

5 Blowdry hair using a Denman brush.
Personalise haircut by point cutting perimeter.

5 Faire le Brushing avec une brosse Denman.
Personaliser la coupe en coupant le périmètre
des cheveux avec les ciseaux à la verticale.

5 Das Haar wird mit Denman Bürste getönt.
Haarschnitt wird dann personalisiert indem
die Aussenkontour point-ult geschmitten wird.

5 Secar el cabello utilizando un cepillo
Denman. Personalizar el corte a punta
de tijera.

5 Si asciugano i capelli a phon usando una
spazzola Denman. Il taglio viene
personalizzato usando la tecnica del "point
cutting" sul perimetro dei capelli.

   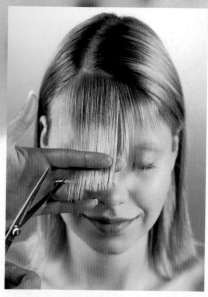

4 Find natural side parting and direct
hair forward at approximately 45° at
a low elevation.

4 Trouver une raie naturelle de côté et
Lisser les cheveux en avant à 45 degrés
en basse élévtion.

4 Der natürliche scheitel wird benutzt, im
45° winkel nach vorne abgehoben und in
einer leichten Abhebung geschnitten.

4 Abrimos la particion natural a un lado y
dirijimos elcabello hacia delante, a
45°con poca elevación.

4 Si trova seziohe naturale laterale e si
portano I capelli in avanti a 45 gradi ad
una bassa elevazione.

6 When hair is dry, point
cut fringe to desired length.

6 Couper la frange avec les
ciseaux à la verticale à une
longueur desirée.

6 Der Pony wird in
trockehem zustand point
cut geschmitten.

6 Cuando el cabello este
seco damos la largura
deseada al flequillo
cortando a punta de tijera.

6 Quando i capelli sono
asciutti, si esegue un "point
cut" alla frangia ad una
lunghezza a piacere.

The technique – Tonal Lightening

Hair prior to colour: Natural Base 7/0 Medium Blonde with previous highlights on ends.

Technique – Eclaircissement de ton

Cheveux avant la coloration: base naturelle 7/0 blond moyen et mèches claires sur les pointes.

Technik – Tonal Lightening

Ausgangsfarbe: Naturton 7/0 mittelblond mit Reststrähnen in den Längen.

Téchnique – Tonal Lightening

Cabelloprevio a la coloración: base natural 7/0 y pre vias nechas en las puntas.

Tecnica – Schiarimento di tono

Capelli prima del colore: base naturale 7/0 biondo medio con colpi di luce sulle punte.

2 Apply the surface colour on the underneath. Color Touch Long Lasting Semi-permanent 7/73 Sienna + 7/47 Tera Rosa with Color Touch Crème Lotion.

2 Colorer la partie au dessous de ces deux sections avec la couleur "surface". Color Touch coloration directe longue durée 7/73 + 7/47 avec Color Touch Lotion Crème.

2 Color Touch 7/73 + 7/47 mit Color Touch Crème Lotion wird nur oberflächlich auf Resthaar aufgetragen.

2 Aplicar color en la superficie de la parte baja . Color Touch Long Lasting semi permanente 7/73 + 7/47 Color Touch/Crème Lotion.

2 Si pone il colore "surface" nella parte sottostante le due sezioni parallele. Color Touch semi-permanente a lunga durata 7/73 + 7/47 con Color Touch Lozione Crema.

12

1 Working with a centre parting a herringbone section was taken from either side of the parting.

1 Tracer une raie centrale et prendre deux sections verticales parallèles de chaque côté de la raie.

1 Mittlescheitel – heringförmige sektioon wird rechts und links des scheitels Abegeteilt.

1 Trabajando con particion central tomar una sección a cada de la linea central.

1 Si pone il colore "surface" nella parte sottostante le due sezioni parallele.

4 When half herringbone section is completed, sections are pivoted on the crown area.

4 Une fois complété la moitié de cette section, les sections sont pivotées sur le point d'éclatement.

4 Es wird um den wirbelpunkt herum gearbeitet. (wirbelpunkt = Drehpunkt)

4 La mitad de la partición es completada, las secciones se pivotean en la zona de la coronilla.

4 Una volta completata meta' di questa sezione, le sezioni vengono portate al centro della calotta.

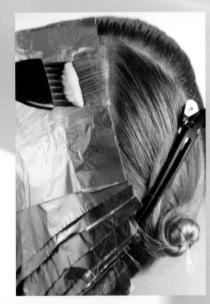

13

3 Using foil, slices are alternated through the herringbone section. Koleston Perfect 12/17 Special Soft Velvet with 12% Welloxon Perfect alternated with Blondor Coco with +6% Welloxon Perfect. The ends were smudged randomly with Color Touch which was used on the under colour to create a two-tone effect.

3 Utiliser des feuilles d'aluminium et prendre des bandes de cheveux dans la section verticale à côté de la raie centrale. Sur ces bandes on alternera deux couleurs: Koleston Perfect 12/17 avec 12% Welloxon Perfect et Blondor Coco avec +6% Welloxon Perfect. Ensuite on colore au hasard les pointes avec Color Touch, le même qui a été employé pour la couleur du dessous, de façon à créer un effet de deux tons de couleur.

3 Die Heringsabteilung wird mit scheibensträhnen bearbeitet. Koleston Perfekt 12.17 mit 12% Welloxon Perfekt wird mit Blondor Coco + 6% Welloxon Perfect abgewechselt. Die Enden werden nur teilweise mit Color Touch (7/73 + 7/47) bestrichen um einen unregelmässigen 2-Ton-Effekt zu kreieren.

3 Utilizando platas, Secciones aluminio son alternadas a través de la particion. Koleston Perfect 12/17 al 12% Welloxon Perfect alternando con Blondor Coco al 6% Welloxon Perfect. Las puntas son suavizadas con Color Touch. Que se utiliza en el color de abajo para crear un efecto de dos tonos.

3 Usando la carta d'alluminio, si prendono sezione verticale dal centro della testa. Due colori vengo poi alternati in queste di capelli: Koleston Perfect 12/17 con 12% Welloxon Perfect e Blondor Coco con +6% Welloxon Perfect. Le punte vengon spennellate a caso con Color Touch che e' stato usato nel sotto colore, in modo da creare un effetto di 2 tonalita.

5 Completed section pattern. Top is block coloured to achieve different tonal effects.

5 Une Fois terminé, la couleur de la partie haute est bloquée, pour obtenir un effet de differentes nuances de couleur.

5 Fertige Abteilung oberkopf wird komplett gefarbt farbreflex zu erzeugen.

5 Completada la sección patrona superior es colereada totalm ente para conseguir diferentes tonalidades.

5 Completata la sezione modello, il colore viene bloccato nella parte alta per ottenere un effetto di toni diversi.

gabriella

Mark Mackelvie
step-by-step cutting

Yumi Dingle
step-by-step colour

14

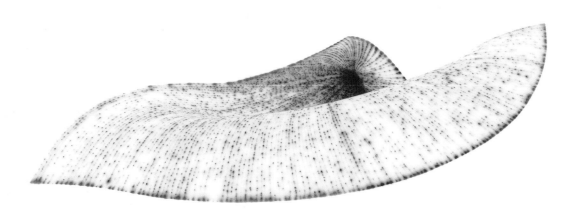

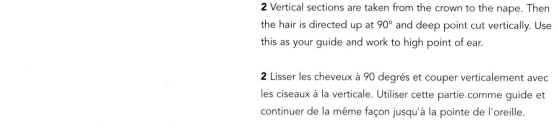

2 Vertical sections are taken from the crown to the nape. Then the hair is directed up at 90° and deep point cut vertically. Use this as your guide and work to high point of ear.

2 Lisser les cheveux à 90 degrés et couper verticalement avec les ciseaux à la verticale. Utiliser cette partie comme guide et continuer de la même façon jusqu'à la pointe de l'oreille.

2 Das Haar wird 90° abgehoben und tief in point cut Technik vertikal geschnitten. Dies wird als Führungslinie benutzt und bis zum höchsten Punkt des ohres bearbeitet.

2 El cabello es elevado con un angulo de 90° y cortado por medio de profundos cortes vertcals. Utilizar esto como guia y conitnuar hasta el ponta alto de la oreja.

2 Si sollevano i capelli a 90 gradi e si esegue un profondo "point cut" verticale. Usando questa parte come guida, si continua a lavorare sino alla punta dell'orecchio.

16

1 A wide profile section is taken from the recession area to behind the crown.

1 Prendre une large Section Profil en partant des tempes jusqu'à arriver derrière le point d'éclatement.

1 Eine Profillinie von den seiten bis unter dem wirbel wird abgeteilt.

1 Se coje una seccion muy ancha desde la zona de las entradas hasta la coronilla.

1 Si prende una larga Sezione Profilo partendo dalle tempie fino ad arrivare dietro la calotta.

5 The hair is overdirected back and point cut.

5 Lisser les cheveux en arrière et couper avec les ciseaux à la verticale.

5 Das Haar wird nach hinten liberzogen und im Pointcut geschnitten.

5 El pelo se dirije hacia atrás y se corta a punta de tijera.

5 I capelli sono poi portati all'indietro e si esegue un "point cut".

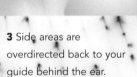
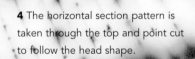

17

3 Side areas are overdirected back to your guide behind the ear.

3 Les cheveux de côté sont lisser à l'arrière vers la partie guide, derrière l'oreille.

3 Die seiten werden zur Führungslinie dem ohr liberzogen.

3 Las zones de los lados se desplazan a la guia detrás de la oreja.

3 Le parti laterali sono portate dietro l'orecchio.

4 The horizontal section pattern is taken through the top and point cut to follow the head shape.

4 Prendre une section horizontale dans la partie haute de la tête.

4 Horizontale Abteilungen auf dem oberkopt werden genommen.

4 Una seccion patrona horizontalmente la parte superior.

4 Si prende una sezione orizzontale lungo la parte alta della testa.

6 The front is overdirected back to the last section behind the ear. Finally, personalise the front to suit.

6 La partie devant est lisser en arrière vers la dernière section derrière l'oreille.

6 Der vordete Bereich wird nach hinten zur letzten Abteilung hinter dem ohr liberzogen.

6 Las parte frontales desplazada hacia atrás, a la ultima sección detras de la oreja.

6 La parte anteriore e' portata indietro verso l'ultima sezione dietro l'orecchio.

1 A diamond section is taken on the top of the head and split into four triangles.

1 Prende une section de la forme d'un losange dans la partie haute de la tête et la separer en quatre triangles.

1 Diamantförmige Sektion wird am oberkopf genommen und in fier Dreiecke abgeteilt.

1 Seha cogido una seccion en forma de diamante en la parte superior de la cabeza y se ha dividido en 4 triangulos.

1 Si prende una sezione a forma di rombo nella parte alta della testa ed in seguito la si suddivide in 4 triangoli.

The Technique – Texturising Colour
Hair prior to colour: Natural Base 6/0 Dark Blonde with previous semi-permanent colour.

Technique – Texturising Colour
Cheveux avant a coloration: base naturelle 6/0 blond foncé et précédente coloration directe.

Technik – Texturising Colour
Ausgangsfarbe: Naturton 6/0 dunkelblond Haar war schon gefärbt.

Técnica – Color Texturizador
Cabello previo a la coloracion base natural 6/0 Dark Blonde.Color previo semi permanente.

Tecnica – Texturising Colour
Capelli prima del colore: base naturale 6/0 biondo scuro e precedente colore semi-permanente.

2 Under colour is applied. Koleston Perfect 4/6 – Rich Damson + 6/6 Sherry Brown with 6% Welloxon Perfect.

2 Mettre le sous- couluer Koleston la couleur du dessous est appliqué Koleston Perfect 4/6 + 6/6 avec 6% Welloxon Perfect.

2 Das Resthaar wird mit Koleston Perfekt 4/6 + 6/6 mit 6% Welloxon Perfekt eingestrichen.

2 El color es aplicado en la parte inferior Koleston Perfect 4/6 + 6/6 al 6% Welloxon Perfect.

2 Il colore si applicanellaparte inferiore Koleston Perfect 4/6+ 6/6 Koleston Perfect 4/6 + 6/6 con 6% Welloxon Perfect.

3 Colour wraps are applied, then slices are taken from each section. Koleston Perfect 6/6 – Sherry Brown with 6% Welloxon Perfect is applied, then Blondor Coco with 6% Welloxon Perfect is applied to the ends.

3 Placer vos papiers meches pour la couleur autour de la tête et prendre des bandes de cheveux de chacune des quatre sections triangulaires. Colorer avec Koleston Perfect 6/6 avec 6% Welloxon Perfect. Ensuite colorer les pointes avec Blondor Colco avec 6% Welloxon Perfect.

3 Dies wird mit TIGI Meche abgedeckt, nun werden von jedem Dreieck Scheibensträhnen genommen. Koleston Perfekt 6/0 mit 6% Welloxon Perfect wird auf die Ansätza aufgetragen. Die Enden werde mit Blondor Coco + 6% Welloxon Perfekt eingestrichen.

3 Particiones paralelas son tomadas de cada sección. Kolestion Perfect 6/6 al 6% Welloxon Perfect es aplicado en las puntas.

3 Cartine apposite per il colore vengono poste attorno al capo, e poi si prendono strati di capelli da ognuna delle 4 sezioni. Si pone dunque Koleston Perfect 6/6 con 6% Welloxon Perfect. In seguito si pone sulle punte Blondor Colco con 6% Welloxon Perfect.

5 The completed application. Slices are taken until no more hair remains.

5 L' application est complétée. On continue à prende des bandes de cheveux jusqu' à couverture total de surface.

5 Es wird zur mitte gearbeutet und dann mit TIGI Meche abgedeckt.

5 Completada la aplicacion, Seguir con las particiones paralelas hasta finalizar con el cabello.

5 Applicazione completata. Si continuano a prendere strati di capelli sino a coprire l'intera superficie.

19

4 Another layer of colour wraps. The next slices taken are Koleston Perfect 6/6 – Sherry Brown is applied. Slices are alternated, one with Blondor Coco on the ends and one without.

4 Mettre une autre couche de papiers pour la couleur et colorer la bande de cheveux suivante avec Koleston Perfect 6/6. On continue ainsi en alternant les couches: une avec Blondor Colco sur les pointes et l'autre sans rien.

4 So wird nun weiter zur mitte hingearbeitet wobei bei der nächsten Abteilung nur Koleston 6/6 verwendet wird. Blondor Coco wird nur bei jeder zweiten Abteilung verwendet.

4 Otra capa de color tomando las siguientes particiones paralelas. Koleston Perfect 6/6 es aplicado Se alternan las particiones/paralelas una con Blondor Coco y otra sin.

4 Si mette poi un altro strato di cartine per il colore e sullo strato successivo di capelli si pone Koleston Perfect 6/6. Si alternano gli strati: uno con Blondor Colco sulle punte ed uno senza.

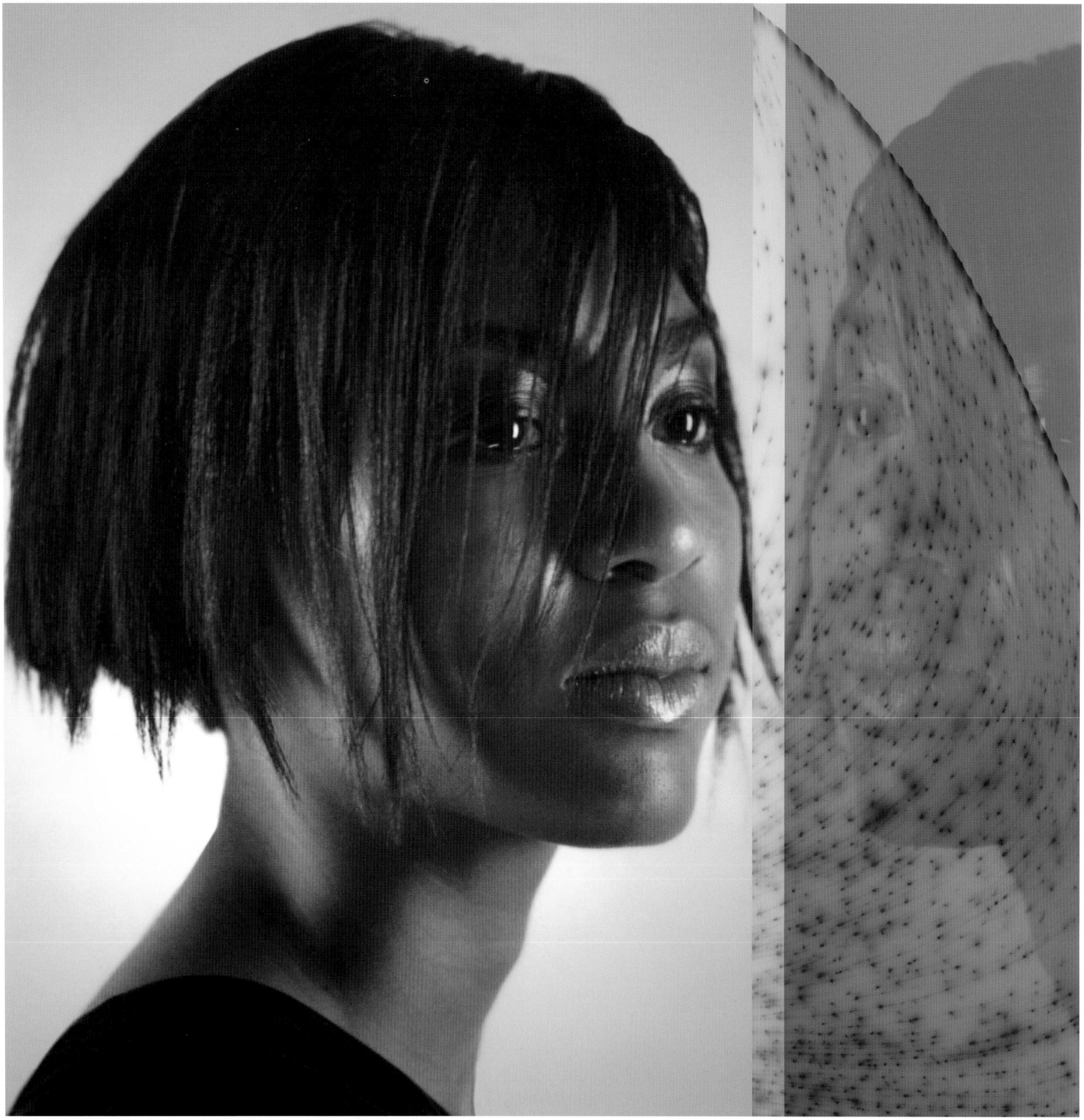

Lanie Reeves
step-by-step cutting
Jackie Grier
step-by-step colour

simone

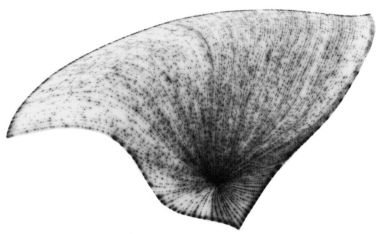

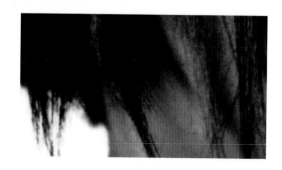

1 A horseshoe section is taken from recession to recession just below the crown.

1 Prendre une section en fer à cheval en allant d'une tempe à l'autre, juste au dessous du point d'éclatement.

1 Hufeisenförmige Abteilung von seite zu seite unterhalb des wirbels.

1 Tomar una sección radial desde la zona de las entradas hasta la parte central posterior, por debajo de la coronilla.

1 Si prende una sezione di capelli a forma di ferro di cavallo da una tempia all'altra, appena al di sotto della calotta.

3 Take the first section vertically and pull out at 90° angle, then pivot through to the nape area.

3 Prendre la première section verticalement et lisser les cheveux à 90 degrés. Ensuite faire pivoter les cheveux au niveau de la nuque.

3 Die erste schnittlinie wird im 90° Winkel vertikal vausgezogen und geschnitten und dann diagonal bis horizontal verfolgt (graduationsartig).

3 Tomar la primera sección vertical estirandola a 90°, girar alrededor, de la zona de la nuca.

3 Si prende la prima sezione verticalmente e si portano i capelli all'infuori ad un'angolazione di 90 gradi, facendo poi perno all'altezza della nuca.

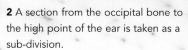

22

2 A section from the occipital bone to the high point of the ear is taken as a sub-division.

2 Prendre une deuxième section en partant de l'os occipital jusqu'à la pointe de l'oreille (comme une subdivision).

2 Zweit-Abteilung am Hinterhauptsknochen zum höchsten Punkt des Ohres.

2 Sección desde el hueeso occipital hasta elpunto alto dela oreja.(Como sub-división).

2 Una seconda sezione va dall'osso occipitale alla punta dell'orecchio (come una suddivisione).

5 Then pull the hair down to the natural fall and point cut.

5 Peigner les cheveux selon leur implantation naturel et couper avec les ciseaux à la verticale.

5 Dann wird das Haar locker nach unten gekämmt und mit point cut geschnitten.

5 Peinar hacia abajo manteniendo la caido natural y cortar mediante tecnica "point cut".

5 In seguito fare scendere i capelli nella loro caduta naturale ed eseguire un "point cut".

23

4 Work a vertical section from crown to nape pulling out at 45°. The section is worked from vertical (at back) through to horizontal at the side front.

4 Travailler sur une section verticale prise du point d'éclatement jusqu'à la nuque. Lisser les cheveux à 90 degrés et couper avec les ciseaux à la verticale. Travailler verticalement sur la section (dans la partie postérieure) et ensuite horizontalement dans la partie laterale et antérieure.

4 Vom wirbel zum Nacken wird eine sektin in 45° Winkel gearbeitet und in point-cut Tecknik bearbeitet. Die sektion wird hinten vertikal und zu den seiten hin horizontal bearbeitet.

4 Trabajar una sección desde la coronilla hacia la nuca estirándola a 45° utilizando tecnica "point cut". La seccion es trabajada de forma vertical (altras) hacia forma horizontal en los laterals del frontal.

4 Si lavora una sezione verticale presa dalla calotta alla nuca, portando fuori i capelli a 45 gradi ed eseguendo un "point cut". La sezione e' lavorata prima verticalmente (nella parte posteriore) e poi orizzontalmente nella parte laterale e anteriore.

The technique – Focal Colour

Hair prior to colour: Natural Base 3/0 Dark Brown, with previous lowlights on ends.

Technique – couleur focale

Cheveux avant coloration: base naturelle 3/0 châtain foncé et précédentes mèches colorées sur les pointes.

Technik – Focal Colour

Ausgangsfarbe: Naturton 3/0 dunkelbraun lowlights in den Längen.

Técnica – Focal Colour

Color del cabello previo al proceso :base natural 3/0 Dark Brown, mechas prevas en las puntas.

Tecnica – Colore focale

Capelli prima del colore: base naturale 3/0 castano scuro e precedenti ciocche colorate sulle punte.

2 The Wella product used, Color Touch Long-lasting Semi-permanent colour 5/5 – Alizarin with Color Touch Intensive Lotion is applied to the remaining hair.

2 Color Touch coloration d'oxydation à longue durée 5/5. On colore la partie restante de cheveux avec Alizarin melangé avec Color Touch Lotion Intensive.

2 Color Touch langanhaltende Tönung 5/5 alizarin mit Intensir Crème Lotion wird auf das Resthaar aufgetragen.

2 Color Touch semi permanente de larga duracion 5/5 con Color Touch Intensive lotion es aplicación por el resto del cabello.

2 Color Touch colore ad ossidazione a lunga durata 5/5 – Ai capelli restanti viene applicato Alizarin con Color Touch lozione intensiva.

24

1 Take a triangular section in the fringe area. This will be the focal point of the haircut.

1 Prende une section de forme triangulaire dans la zone de la frange. Celle-ci deviendra le point central de la coupe.

1 Eine Drereckssektion wird im Ponybereich abgeteitt.

1 Sección triangular tomada en el area del flequillo.

1 Si prende una sezione a forma triangolare nella zona della frangia. Questa sara' la parte centrale del taglio.

4 Triangular section is coloured in slices to ensure hair is thoroughly covered. Koleston Perfect 77/44 Vibrant Flame Red with12% Welloxon Perfect.

4 On colore la section de forme triangulaire en faisant des couches, afin que la couleur soit uniformement distribuée sur toute la surface des cheveux. Koleston Perfect 77/44 avec 12% Welloxon Perfect.

4 Dreieckssektion wird scheibenweise aufgetragen um perfekte Abdeckung zu erreichen, Koleston Perfekt 77/44 mit 12% Welloxon Perfekt.

4 La particion triangular es coloreada cojiendo pequenas secciones para asegurarnos de que el cabello está completamante cubierto. Koleston Perfect 77/44 al 12% Welloxon Perfect.

4 La sezione triangolare viene colorata a strati, per fare in modo che il colore venga uniformemente distribuito su tutti i capelli. Koleston Perfect 77/44 con 12% Welloxon Perfect.

3 Completed Color Touch application.

3 L'application Color Touch est complétée.

3 Nach dem Auftragen von Color Touch.

3 Completada la aplicicón de Color Touch.

3 Applicazione Color Touch completata.

5 Completed application.

5 Application complétée.

5 Farbe nach dem Auftragen.

5 Completada la aplicicion.

5 Applicazione completata.

Christian Mascolo
step-by-step cutting
Julie Gurr
step-by-step colour

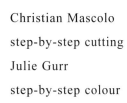

katie

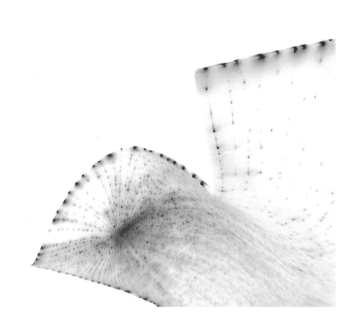

2 Make a diagonal forward sectioning pattern, bringing all sections down through the comb. Then cut the line parallel to the section pattern.

2 Lisser les cheveux vers le bas en differentes sections en traçant avec le peigne des lignes diagonales. Les sections sont parallèles pour aligner la coupe.

2 Vom mittelscheitel werden diagonale sektionen abgeteilt und das Haar wird unter dem kamm geschmitten. Die Abteilungen liegen parallel zur schmittlinie.

2 Particiónes/diagonales llevando todas las secciones hacia abajo a través del peine. Contnuamos con secciones paralelas a la primera.

2 I capelli sono portati verso il basso in diverse sezioni, usando il pettine e tracciando linee diagonali in avanti. Le sezioni sono parallele per allineare il taglio.

1 Section the crown to the high point of the ear.

1 Faire une séperation des cheveux en partant du point d'eclatement jusqu'aux oreilles.

1 Abteilung vom wirbel zum höchstem Punkt des Ohres.

1 Sección desde la coronilla hasta la parte alta de la orega.

1 I capelli sono separati partendo dalla calotta fino alla punta delle orecchie.

4 Personalise by pulling hair down to natural fall and slicing.

4 Peigner les cheveux selon leur pli naturel et personaliser en coupant avec les ciseaux à la verticale.

4 Der Haarschmitt wird personalisiert indem das Haar natürlich nach unten gezogen wird und mit Slicing-Technik bearbeitet wird.

4 Personalizar peinando el cabello con caida natural a punta de tijera.

4 Seguendo la caduta naturale dei capelli, personalizzare il taglio eseguendo un "point cutting".

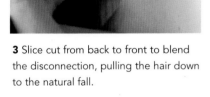

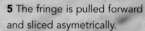

3 Slice cut from back to front to blend the disconnection, pulling the hair down to the natural fall.

3 En peignant, faire un effilage glissé en partant de l'arrière et en se dirigeant en avant, de façon à donner un équilibre à la coupe.

3 Von hinten wird das Haar mit Slicing-Technik mit den seiten verbunden. Das Haar wird natürlich locker gekämmt.

3 Cortar deslizando desde atrás hacia delante para unir la desconexión peinando el cabello con caida natural.

3 Si sfilano i capelli partendo dal retro e proseguendo nella parte anteriore in modo da renderli pari, e facendoli scendere nel loro modo naturale.

5 The fringe is pulled forward and sliced asymetrically.

5 Amener la france devant et faire un effilage glissé asymétrique.

5 Der Pony wird nach vorne gebracht und assymetrisch geshnitten.

5 El flequillo es peinando hacia delante y cortado asimetricamente des lizando la tijera.

5 La frangia viene portata in avanti e sfilata in modo asimmetrico.

1 The halo section pattern is taken, then zig-zagged to enable the colour to blend. Below this section, four panels are taken.

1 Faire des raies zigzag dans la partie haute du point d'éclatement pour permettre à la couleur de bien se mélanger. Ensuite prendre quatre bandes de cheveux au dessous de cette section.

1 Kreisförmige Abteilung am Oberkopf, zick-zack Abteilung um ein Einblenden der Farbe zu ermöglichen. Unterhalb werden 4 Abschnitte genommen.

1 Sección patrón en forma de aureola dividida en 4 paneles con zig-zag para difuminar los colores.

1 Nella zona alta della calotta si fanno delle sezioni a zig zag per permettere al colore di mescolarsi. Si prendono poi quattro strisce di capelli al di sotto di questa sezione.

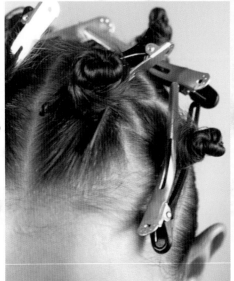

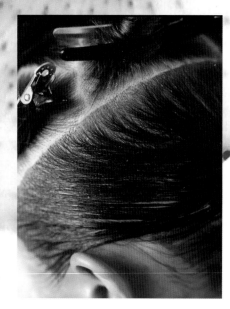

The technique – Panelling
Hair prior to colour: Natural Base 6/0 Dark Blonde. No previous colour.

Technique – Panelling
Cheveux avant coloration: base naturelle 6/0 blond foncé. Aucune couleur précédente.

Technik – Panelling
Ausgangsfarbe: Naturton 6/0 dunkelblonde unbehandeltes Haar.

Técnia – Panelling
Cabello previo a coloracion: base natural 6/0 Dark Blonde

Tecnica – Panelling
Capelli prima del colore: base naturale 6/0 biondo scuro. Nessun colore precedente.

2 The remaining hair below these sections is coloured with Color Touch Long-lasting Semi-permanent 6/37 Indian Bronze with Color Touch Crème Lotion.

2 Colorer les cheveux qui restent au dessous de ces sections avec Color Touch 6/37 coloration directe à longue durée avec Color Touch Lotion Crème.

2 Das Resthaar wird mit langannaltender Color Touch Tönung 6/37 mit Color Touch Crème Lotion getärbt.

2 El pelo de la parte inferior de esta sección es coloreado con Color Touch Long Lasting semi permanante 6/37 con Color Touch Crème Lotion.

2 I rimanenti capelli al di sotto di queste sezioni vengono colorati con Color Touch 6/37 semi-permanente a lunga durata con Color Touch Lozione Crema.

3 Working on each panel, slices are taken using colour wraps. Each slice was alternated with three colours to create panels of colour. Color Touch 6/37 Indian Bronze with Crème Lotion, Koleston Perfect 88/43 Vibrant Celtic Copper with 9% + Blondor Coco with 6% Welloxon Perfect.

3 En employant des papiers pour la couleur, prendre des mèches de cheveux de chaque bande. Colorer chaque mèche en alternant 3 couleurs, pour créer différentes nuances. Color Touch 6/37 avec Lotion Crème, Koleston Perfect 88/43 avec 9% + Blondor Coco avec 6% Welloxon Perfect.

3 An allen Abschnitten wird mit Tigi Meche gearbeitet. Jede Stähne wird mit 3 Farben eingestrichen: Color Touch 6/37 mit Crème Lotion Koleston Perfekt 88/43 mit 9% Blondor Coco mit 6% Welloxon Perfekt.

3 Tranajamos secciones paralelas en cada panel. Cada paralela as alternada con tres colores para clear paneles de color. Color Touch 6/37 con Crème Lotion, Koleston Perfect 88/43 con 9% + Blondor coco 6% Welloxon Perfect.

3 Ciocche di capelli vengono prese da ogni striscia usando cartine apposite per il colore. Ogni ciocca di capelli viene alternata con 3 diversi colori per creare strisce di colori. Color Touch 6/37 con Lozione Crema, Koleston Perfect 88/43 con 9% + Blondor coco con 6% Welloxon Perfect.

5 Hair was personalised by channel cutting.

5 Les cheveux ont ete personnalises pas channel coupe.

5 Das haar wurde durch kanalschneiden texturiert.

5 Personelisa el corte usando la technica 'channel'.

5 Il taglio e stato personalizato usando il 'channel cutting'.

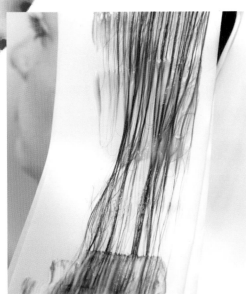

31

4 Each slice colour was placed in different positions to create different panels.

4 Sur chaque mèche on place la couleur dans des positions différentes, pour qu'on puisse obtenir des différentes nuances.

4 Jede Strähne wird verschieden abwechselnd gefärbt um unterschiedliche Schattierungen zu kreieren.

4 Cada sección paralela tiene los colores en diferentes posiciones para crear diferentes paneles.

4 Il colore di ogni ciocca di capelli viene posto in posizioni diverse per creare diversi pannelli di colore.

5 The panels completed. Color Touch 6/37 Indian Bronze was applied to the halo section on the top.

5 Une fois qu'on a terminé de colorer toutes les bandes de cheveux, on colore aussi la zone du point d'éclatement avec Color Touch 6/37.

5 Auf die kriesformige Abteilung wird Colour Touch 6/37 aufgetragen

5 Panelas completados. Color Touch 6/37 ha sido apliado en la sección en forma de aureola superior.

5 Strisce di colore completate. Color Touch 6/37 viene poi posto anche nella zona della calotta.

francesca

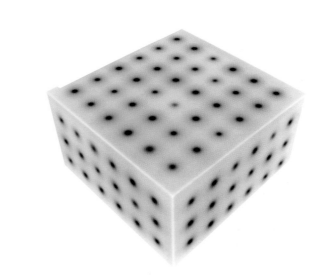

Christian Mascolo
step-by-step cutting
Justin Smith
step-by-step colour

2 Comb the hair to the natural fall. Then hold through the fingers and razor the baseline.

2 Peigner les cheveux selon leur implantation naturel et en le seviant entre les doigts, couper la ligne de base au rasior.

2 Die Basislinie wird natürlich locker gekämmt und mit messer geschnitten.

2 Peinar elcabello con caido natural, sujetar conlos dedos y cortar a navaja la largura total.

2 Si pettinano i capelli seguendo la loro caduta naturale e, tenendoli fra le dita, si taglia la linea di base con un rasoio.

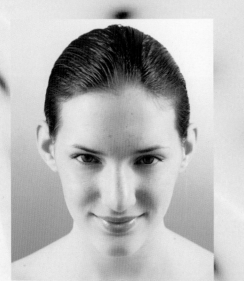   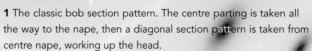

1 The classic bob section pattern. The centre parting is taken all the way to the nape, then a diagonal section pattern is taken from centre nape, working up the head.

1 Séparer les cheveux selon le modèle classique du carré. Tracer la raie centrale jusqu'à arriver à la nuque. Ensuite, en partant du centre de la nuque, tracer deux sections diagonales et monter vers le haut de la tête.

1 Abteilungen des Classic Bobs. Mittelscheitel bis hin zum Nacken. Diagonale sektionen werden zur seite hingezogen.

1 Sección patron de "clasic bob". Raya en medio hasta la nuca, secciones diagonales desede el centro de la nuca trabajando hacia la parte superior de la cabeza.

1 Suddivisione del capelli seguendo il modello del classico taglio paso. La sezione centrale viene fatta scendere sino all nuca e poi dal centro della nuca si tracciano deu sezioni diagonali e si prosegue in questo modo salendo verso l'alto.

4 Use the guide from the base line and pull the hair up at 90° from the top of the head. Then slice the top area, maintaining the front perimeter length.

4 En utilisant comme guide la ligne de base, lisser les cheveux de la partie haute de la tête à 90 degrés et faire un effilage glissé, en gardant la longueur du périmètre antérieur.

4 Die Basislinie dient las Fühurngspunkt und wird mit 90° Winkel geraderausgekämmt und mit "slice cutting" bearbeitet wobei die Läange im Kontourbereich erhalten bleibt.

4 Utilizar la guia de la largura total y elevar el cabello a 90° de la parte superior de la cabeza. Cortar la zona superior manteniendo la seccion frontal.

4 Usando come guida la linea di base, si portano i capelli della parte alta della testa fuori a 90 gradi e si sfilano, cosí da formate un angolo tra il perimitro e la nuova sezione.

 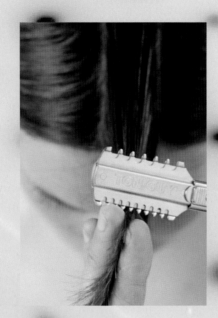  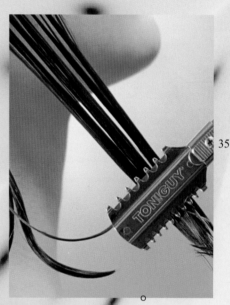

3 Follow from centre back through to recession, working parallel to your previous section and combing hair to the natural fall.

3 On commence par la partie postérieure et on continue vers la zone des tempes, en travaillant parallèlement à la section précédente. On peigne les cheveux selon leur pli naturel.

3 Die seiten werden verbunden indem das Haar parallel zur letzten Abteilung natürlich gekämmt und geschnitten wird.

3 Seguir desde el centro de la parte de atras hacia la zona de las entradas, trabajando en paralelo a las secciones anteriores y peinando el cabello con caida natural.

3 Si procede dalla parte posteriore verso la zona delle tempie, lavorando parallelamente alla sezione precedente e pettinando i capelli in modo da seguire la loro caduta naturale.

5 Pull the hair forward at 45° and slice the perimeter shape.

5 Lisser les cheveux vers l'exterieur, à 45 degrés et faire un effilage glissé à la forme du périmètre.

5 Das Haar im Vorderbereich wird im 45° Winkel herausgekämmt und mit dem messer geschnitten.

5 Dirigir el cabello hacia delante a 45° y crear la forna del perimetro.

5 Si portano i capelli all'infuori a 45 gradi e si sfila la forma del perimetro.

Technique – Veiling

Hair prior to colour: Natural Base 7/0 Medium Blonde with previous highlights on ends.

Technique – Voiler

Cheveux avant coloration: base naturelle 7/0 blond moyen avec des précédentes mèches claires sur les pointes.

Technik – Veiling

Ausgangsfarbe: Naturton 7/0 mittelblond mit Strähnen in den Längen.

Tecnica – Veiling

Cabello previo a coloración: base natural 7/0 medio blonde mas previas mechas en las puntas.

Tecnica – Velare

Capelli prima del colore: base naturale 7/0 biondo medio piu' precedenti colpi di luce sulle punte.

3 Starting at the point of the triangle a foil is used and then slices are taken, three colours are placed on each slice to create a gradation of colour. Koleston Perfect 7/7 Warm Velvet Blonde with 6% Welloxon Perfect, 9/93 Soft Cedre with 9% Welloxon Perfect + 12/16 Special Soft Ash with 12% Welloxon Perfect.

3 Partir de la pointe du triangle, placer une feuille de papier aluminium et prendre des mèches de cheveux. Colorer chaque mèche avec 3 couleurs differents, pour créer un effet de gradation de couleurs. Koleston Perfect 7/7 avec 6% Welloxon Perfect, 9/93 avec 9% Welloxon Perfect + 12/16 avec 12% Welloxon Perfect.

3 Scheibensträhnen werden am Dreieck aufgefragen um eine graduationsartige Farbe zu erzengen Koleston Perfekt 7/7 mit 6% Welloxon Perfekt, 9/93 mit 9% Welloxon Perfekt und 12/16 mit 12% Welloxon Perfekt.

3 Empezando en el punto del triángulo se coloca un aluminio y se toman particiones paraelas,tres colores son aplicados en cada partición para crear una graduación de color. Koleston Perfect 7/7 al 6% Welloxon Perfect, 9/93 al 9% Welloxon Perfect +12/16 al 12% Welloxon Perfect.

3 Partendo dalla punta del triangolo, si pone un foglio di carta alluminio e si prendono strati di capelli. Su ogni strato di capelli vengono posti 3 colori per creare un effetto di gradazione di colore. Koleston Perfect 7/7 biondo porpora con 6% Welloxon Perfect, 9/93 con 9% Welloxon Perfect + 12/16 con 12% Welloxon Perfect.

36

1 A triangular section is taken on the top of the head. This is the focal point to create a veil of colour.

1 Tracer une section triangulaire dans la partie haute de la tête. Ceci sera le point central pour créer un voil de couleur.

1 Dreiecksabteikung wird am oberkopf genommen. Dies ist der Focuspunkt dieser Haarfarbe und kreiert eine Art "Schleier".

1 Seccio¢n triangular en la parte superior de la cabeza. Este es el punto de foco para crear un velo de color.

1 Si prende una sezione triangolare nella parte alta della testa. Questo e' il punto centrale per creare un velo di colore.

2 The underneath is coloured using Wella's Color Touch Long-Lasting Semi-permanent colour 6/75 Warm Heather with Color Touch Intensive Lotion.

2 Colorer la partie au dessous du triangle avec Color Touch bruyère 6/75 coloration directe à longue durée avec Color Touch Lotion Intensive.

2 Unterhalb der sektion wird Color Touch laug anhaltende Tönung 6/75 mit Color Touch Intensive Lotion aufgebragen.

2 La parte inferior es coloreada utilizando Color Touch semi permanente de larga duración 6/75 con Color Touch Intensive Lotion.

2 Il resto del capelli verranno colorati usando Color Touch color erica 6/75 semi-permanente a lunga durata con Color Touch Lozione Intensiva.

5 The completed application of a veil of colour is achieved with different depths and tones.

5 Une fois que l'application est complétée, on obtient un voil de couleur avec différents tons et profondeurs.

5 Farbe nach dem Auftragen – schleierartige. Form mit verschiedenen Tönen und Farb-relexen.

5 Completada la aplicacion, un velo de color es conseguido con diferentes alturas y tonos.

5 Una volta completata l'applicazione, si ottiene un velo di colore con diverse profondita' e toni.

4 Work your way forward to the base of triangle, graduating your colours and alternating their postions.

4 Continuer la coloration vers la base du triangle, en graduant la couleur et en alternant ses positions.

4 Es wird nach vorne weitergearbeitet, indem die Farben abwechselnd aufgetragen werden.

4 Trabajar hacia delante hasta la base del traiangulo graduando el color y alternando las posiciones.

4 Si procede l'applicazione in avanti verso la base del triangolo, graduando il colore e alternando le sue posizioni.

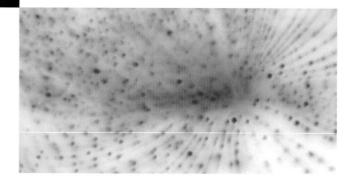

Ian Daburn
step-by-step cutting
Julie Gurr
step-by-step colour

irene

1 Blowdry the hair straight and divide with a centre parting.

1 Sécher les cheveux avec un séchoir en les lissant et tracer une raie centrale.

1 Das Haar wird glattgefönt und im mittelscheitel gekämmt.

1 Secar el pelo liso y dividirlo con raya en medio.

1 Si asciugano i capelli a phon allisciandoli e li si separa con una linea centrale.

3 Take a profile line, which is a section about an inch wide from front to back. Pull the hair straight up and cut by slicing.

3 Tracer la Ligne Profil. Il s'agit d'une section de cheveux, large plus au moins 3cm, allant du front vers la nuque. Lisser les cheveux vers le haut et faire un effilage glissé.

3 Eine ca. 3 cm dicke Profillinie wird von stirn zum Nacken abgeteilt. Das Haar wird vertikal rausgekämmt und mit Slicing Technik geschnitten.

3 Tomar una linea de perfil, que es una sección de aproximadamente 2.5cm de grosor desde elfrontal hacia atras. Elevar el cabello y cortar mediante técnica "slicing".

3 Si prende una sezione di 3cm, nel centro della testa I capelli seranno poi pettinati nei loro 90°. E sarro poi tagliati usando la sfilatura.

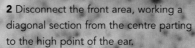

2 Disconnect the front area, working a diagonal section from the centre parting to the high point of the ear.

2 Séparer la partie antérieure de celle postérieure en traçant une ligne diagonale qui part de la raie centrale pour arriver à la pointe de l'oreille.

2 Desconectar el area frontal por medio de una seccio¢n diagonal tomada desda la partición central hasta el punto alto de la oreja.

2 Diagonale Abteilungen werden vom mittelschitel zum our hin genommen.

2 Si sepera la parte antreiore da quella posteriore tracciando una linea diagonale che va da orecchio a orecchio passando per il centro.

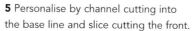

5 Personalise by channel cutting into the base line and slice cutting the front.

5 Personaliser en coupant avec les ciseaux à la verticale sur la ligne de base (éliminer du poids aux cheveux en gardant la longueur) et en faisant un effilage glissé dans la partie antérieure.

5 Der vordere Bereich und die Basislinie wird mit channelcutting personalisiert.

5 Personalizar utilizando tecnica "channel cutting" la largura total y cortar la parte frontal mediante técnica "slicing".

5 Si personalizza il taglio usando la tecnica "channel cutting" sulla linea di base (eliminare peso al capello ma mantenendo la lunghezza) e sfilando la parte anteriore.

4 Pull up at 90° from the top of the head. Then cut a square line by slicing.

4 Ensuite, lisser les cheveux vens l'exterieur à 90 degrés, en partant de la partie haute de la tête. Couper une ligne recte avec un effilage glissé.

4 Haar wird vom Oberkoft im 90° Winkel rausgezogen. Eine Linie wird mit Slicing Technik geschnitten.

4 Estirar el cabello a 90` de la parte superior de la cabeza. Cortar una linea recta con la técnica "slicing".

4 In seguito si portano i capelli all'infuori a 90 gradi, partendo dalla parte alta della testa. Si taglia una linea retta sfilando.

Technique – Hidden Lightening

Hair prior to colour: Natural Base 7/0 Medium Blonde, previous highlights on ends.

Technique – Eclaircissement Caché

Cheveux avant la coloration: base naturelle 7/0 blond moyen, précédentes mèches claires sur les pointes.

Tachnik – Hidden Lightening

Ausgangsfarbe: Naturton 7/0 mittelblond Strähnen in den Längen.

Técnica – Hidden Lightening

Cabello previo a la coloracion. Base natural 7/0 Rubio medio, mechas previas en las puntas.

Tecnica – Schiarimento Camuffato

Capelli prima del colore: base naturale 7/0 biondo medio, precedenti colpi di luce sulle punte.

2 Working firstly on the rectangular section, woven lights are worked through it. Colours are alternated, Koleston Perfect 12/16 Special Soft Ash with 12% Welloxon Perfect + 9/93 Soft Cendre with12% Welloxon Perfect.

2 Commencer avec la section rectangulaire pour créer un effet de lumières entrelacées. On alterne les couleurs: Koleston Perfect 12/16 avec 12% Welloxon Perfect + 9/93 avec 12% Welloxon Perfect.

2 Dreieckssektion wird am oberkopf genommen bei dem eine spitze nach vorne zeigt. Underhalb werden kleinere Dreiecke und vierecke abdgeteilt. Dies wird der Focus punkt dieser Frisur.

2 Trabajando primero en la sección rectangular se cojen particiones en Zig-Zag. Los colores son alternados, Koleston Perfect 12/16 al 12% Welloxon Perfect 9/93 al 12% Welloxon Perfect.

2 Si inizia con la sezione rettangolare e si crea un effetto di luci intrecciate. I colori vengono alternati, usando Koleston Perfect 12/16 con 12% Welloxon Perfect + 9/93 con 12% Welloxon Perfect.

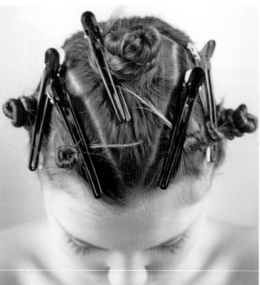

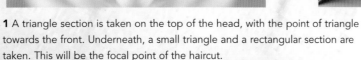

1 A triangle section is taken on the top of the head, with the point of triangle towards the front. Underneath, a small triangle and a rectangular section are taken. This will be the focal point of the haircut.

1 Prendre une section triangulaire dans la partie haute de la tête, a c la pointe du triangle vers le front. Dans la partie au dessous ensuite tracer deux autres sections plus petite, une triangulaire et l'autre rectangulaire. Celle-ci sera la partie centrale de la coupe.

1 Dreieckssektion wird am oberkopf genommen bei dem eine spitze nach vorne zeigt. Underhalb werden kleinere Dreiecke und vierecke abdgeteilt. Dies wird der Focus punkt dieser Frisur.

1 Se coje una sección triangular en la parte superior, la punta del triangulo esta situada en la parte frontal. En la parte inferior se situa una seccion triangular y otra rectangular, este será el punto de enfoque del corte de pelo

1 Si prende una sezione triangolare nella parte alta della testa, con la punta del triangolo diretta verso la fronte. Nella parte sottostante, si prendono poi altre due piccole sezioni, una a forma triangolare e l'altra rettangolare. Questa sara' la parte centrale del taglio.

4 Colour is applied to the back and the top triangle: Colour Touch Long lasting Semi-permanent 6/35 Rich Bronze with Color Touch Crème Lotion.

4 Colorer la partie postérieure et le grand triangle dans la partie haute de la tête avec Color Touch 6/35 coloration directe à longue durée bronze vif avec Colour Touch Lotion Crème.

4 Auf das Resthaar und das obere Dreiech wird langhaltende Color Touch 6/35 mit Color Touch Crème Lotion aufgetragen.

4 El color es aplicado en la parte de atras y en el triangulo superior semi permanente de larga duración 6/35 con Color Crème Lotion.

4 La parte posteriore e il grande triangolo nella parte alta della testa vengono colorati con Color Touch 6/35 semi-permanente a lunga durata con Color Touch Lozione Crema.

6 The Climazon Millenium enables us to achieve optimum results when developing.

6 "Climazon Millenium" permet d'obtenir des résultats optimaux pendant le temps de pause de la couleur.

6 Climazon Millenium ermöglicht eine optimale Entwicklung der Haarfarbe.

6 El Climazon Millenium nos permite obtener los resultados mientras transcurre el tiempo de exposición.

6 "Climazon Millenium" permette di raggiungere risultati ottimali durante il periodo di posa del colore.

  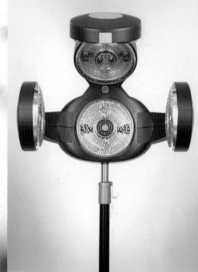

3 After the rectangular sections are completed, work through the smaller triangle. This is worked on both sides.

3 Après avoir complété la section rectangulaire, on passe à la petite section triangulaire. La même technique est employée sur les deux côtés.

3 Nun wird mit den Dreiecken un beiden seiten gearbeitet.

3 Una vez la sección rectangular es completada, trabajar por el triangulo pequeño, repetir en ambos lados.

3 Dopo aver completato la sezione rettangolare, si procede con la piccola sezione triangolare. La stessa tecnica viene usata in entrambi i lati.

5 Completed application. The underneath at the front will be the focal point of the colour.

5 Application complétée. La partie basse antérieure sera le point central de la couleur.

5 Farbe nach dem Auftragen Strähnen sind "versteckt" und Bewgung des Haars sichtbar – Focuspunkt der Frisur.

5 Completa la aplicación de la parte inferior del frontal será el punto de foco del color.

5 Applicazione completata. La parte bassa anteriore sara' la parte centrale del colore.

iesha

Drew Foster
step-by-step cutting
Kate Williams
step-by-step colour

2 Pull the hair down to the natural fall. Point cut a square line.

2 Peigner les cheveux selon leur implantation natural et couper une ligne recte avec les ciseaux à la verticale.

2 Das Haar wird locker gekämmt und in einer linie Im "point cut" geschnitten.

2 Pienamos hacia abajo del pelo con caida natural. Cortar a punta de tijera (point cating) una linea recta.

2 Si fanno scendere I capelli nella loto caduta naturale e si taglia una linea retta usando la tecnica del "point cut".

46

1 Start with the classic bob section pattern. From the centre parting take diagonal sections.

1 Séparer les cheveux selon le modèle classique du carré. En partant de la raie centrale, créer une autre section en traçant deux lignes diagonales.

1 Abteilungen des Classic Bobs. Diagonale Abteilungen werden vom mittel scheitel benützt.

1 Desde el centro detrás de la cabeza hacemos dos secciones diagonales.

1 Suddivisione dei capelli seguendo il modello del taglio pato.. Partendo dalla linea centrale si crea un'altra sezione tracciando due linee diagonali.

3 Disconnect the front area and work horizontal sections, pulling hair down to the natural fall then point cut a square line.

3 Séparer la partie antérieure du reste des cheveux et travailler sur des sections horizontales. Peigner les cheveux selon leur implimantation naturel et couper une ligne recte avec les ciseaux à la verticale.

3 Der vordere Bereich wird abdgeteilt, horizontale Abteilungen werden locker vuntergekämmt und in point-cut zu einer geraden linie geschnitten.

3 Desconectar el area frontal y trabajar secciones horizontales peinando el pelo hacia abajo con caido natural y cortar a punta de tijera una linea recta.

3 Si separa la parte anteriore dal resto dei capelli e si lavora su sezioni orizzontali, facendo scendere i capelli nel loro modo naturale e tagliando una linea retta usando la tecnica del "point cut".

4 Central vertical section pattern is taken from the crown out at 90° from the occipital bone. Point cut the corner using a base line as a guide to length.
5 Continue the section pattern to the ear then overdirect to maintain the weight at the back of the ear.

4 Prendre une section verticale dans la partie centrale de la tête, en partant du point d'éclatement. Etirer les cheveux de la zone occipitale en dehors à 90 degrés et couper l'angle avec les ciseaux à la verticale, en utilisant une ligne de base comme guide pour la longueur.
5 En se diregeant vers l'oreille, amener les cheveux à l'arrière pour maintenir le poids derrière l'oreille.

4 Vertikale Abteilungen werden im 90° Winkel abgehoben und zum Himterhauptknochen vuntergearbeitet wobei die Basislinie als Führugspunkt dient.
5 Vertikal wird auch zum Ohr hingearbeitet, die seiten werden jedoch zur überzogen um Gewicht beizu behlten.

4 Tomar una sección central vertiacl como patrón desde la coronilla a 90° del occipital. Cortaa punta de tijera la esquina utilizando la largura total como referncia.
5 Continuar la sección patrón hasta la oreja. Desplazar hacia atrás para mantener el peso detrás de la oreja.

4 Un'altra sezione viene presa verticalmente nella parte centrale della testa, partendo dalla calotta. I capelli vengono portati all'infuori a 90 gradi nella zona occipitale. Si esegue un "point cut" nell'angolo, usando una linea di base come guida per la lunghezza.
5 Procedendo verso l'orecchio, i capelli vengono portati all'indietro in modo da mantenere il peso dietro l'orecchio.

6 Take the central section from the crown to the front hairline and elevate to 90°. Use the length at the crown as a guide, then pull up at 90° and point cut a square line.

6 Prendre une section centrale qui part du point d'éclatement et arrive au front. Etirer les cheveux vers le haut à 90 degrés et, en se servant de la longueur du point d'éclatement comme guide, couper une ligne recte avec les ciseaux à la verticale.

6 Eine Abteilung vom Wirbel zur stirn wird genommen und im 90° Winkel vausgekämmt. Die länge am Wirbel dient als Führungspunkt und eime linie wird im point cut geschnitten.

6 Tomar una partición central desde la coronilla hasta la raya frontal elevarla a 90°, utilaizar la largura de la coconilla como guia de longuitud. Elevar a 90'y cortar a punta de tijera una linea recta.

6 Si prende una sezione centrale partendo dalla calotta arrivando fino all'attaccatura anteriore. I capelli vengono portati verso l'alto ad un'angolazione di 90 gradi e, usando la lunghezza del punto della calotta come guida, tagliare una linea retta con la tecnica del "point cut".

1 A diamond section is taken on the top of the head and split into four triangular sections.

1 Prende une section de la forme d'un losange dans la partie haute de la tête et la separer en quatre triangles.

1 Diamantförmige sektion wird am oberkopf genommen und in vier Dreiecke abgeteitt.

1 Se coje una sección de diamante en la parte superior de la cabeza y se divide en cuatro secciones triangulares.

1 Si prende una sezione a forma di rombo nella parte alta della testa e poi la si suddivide in quattro sezioni triangolari.

  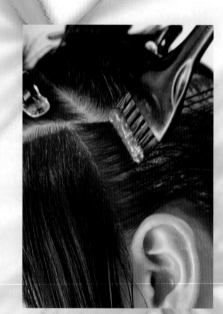

48

Technique – Perimeter Lightening
Hair prior to colour: Natural Base 6/0 Dark Blonde.

Technique – Eclaircissement du périmètre
Cheveux avant coloration: base naturelle 6/0 blond foncé.

Tachnik – Perimeter Lightening
Ausgangsfarbe Naturton 6/0 dunkelblond.

Técnica – Perimeter Lightening
Cabello previo a la coloración base 6/0 Dark Blonde.

Tecnica – Schiarimento del perimetro
Capelli prima del colore: base naturale 6/0 biondo scuro.

2 Colour is applied to the roots of the underneath. Koleston Perfect 77/44 Vibrant Flame Red with 6% Welloxon Perfect.

2 Colorer la racine des cheveux de la partie au dessous du losange. Koleston Perfect 77/44 avec 6% Welloxon Perfect.

2 Auf die Ansätza des Reshaares wird Koleston Perfekt 77/44 mit 6% Welloxon Perfekt aufgetragen.

2 El color se aplica en las raices de la parte inferior. Koleston Perfect 77/44 al 6% Welloxon Perfect.

2 Si pone il colore alla radice dei capelli della zona sottostante questa sezione. Koleston Perfect 77/44 con 6% Welloxon Perfect.

3 The colour is then applied to the mid-lengths and ends on the underneath section using Koleston Perfect 77/44 Vibrant Flame Red with 9% Welloxon Perfect. A higher developer is used on the ends to level the colour.

3 Ensuite on colore aussi le milieu de la longueur des cheveux et les pointes. Koleston Perfect 77/44 avec 9% Welloxon Perfect. Sur les pointes on employera un activateur plus fort pour rendre la courleur uniforme.

3 Nun wird die Farbe auf die Längen und spitzen aufgetragen. Spitzen aufgetragen. Es wird 77/44 mit 9% Welloxon Perfekt verwendet. Ein höherer Prozentlevel wird verwendet um eine gliechmässige Farbe zu eizielen.

3 El color es aplicado ahora en medios y puntas 77/44 a 9% Welloxon Perfect. Un revelador más alto es utilizado en las puntas para igualar el color.

3 Il colore viene poi posto anche a meta' della lunghezza dei capelli e sulle punte. Koleston Perfect 77/44 con 9% Welloxon Perfect. Sulle punte viene usato un piu' alto attivatore per rendere il colore uniforme.

5 Color Fresh Semi-permanent colour 5/0 Light Brown mixed with 6/7 Rich Velvet.

5 Color Fresh châtain clair 5/0 coloration directe melangé avec 6/7.

5 Color Fresh leichte Tönung 5/0 und 6/7.

5 Color Fresh color semi permanente 5/0 mezclado con 6/7.

5 Colour Fresh castano chiaro 5/0 semi-permanente mescolato con 6/7.

49

4 The foil was placed to protect the underneath section and then hair was splayed over the foil. Color Fresh was applied with a sponge from the roots, merging out towards the ends on the surface.

4 Placer des feuilles de papier aluminium pour protéger la partie qu'on vient de colorer. Répandre les cheveux de la partie haute sur toute la surface des feuilles d'aluminium, en les separant en différentes mèches. Appliquer la couleur Color Fresh avec une éponge, en partant de la racine des cheveux pour descendre vers la surface des pointes.

4 Nun wird der untere Teil mit Folie abgedeckt und das obere Haar drübergelegt. Color Fresh wird nun mit einem schwamm aufgetragen. Die spitzen werden nur unregelmässig bearbeitet.

4 Se colocan aluminios para proteger la sección inferior y el resto del cabello se co, loca sobre los aluminios. Color Fresh es aplicado mediante la esponja desde las raices hasta las puntas.

4 Fogli di alluminio vengono posti per proteggere la parte appena colorata. I capelli della parte alta vengono distribuiti su tutta la superficie dei fogli d'alluminio, separandoli in diverse ciocche. Con una spugna si pone poi il colore Color Fresh partendo dalla radice dei capelli proseguendo via via sulla superficie delle punte.

jamie

Christian Mascolo
step-by-step cutting
June Graham
step-by-step colour

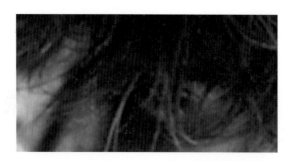

51

1 The hair is thick in texture and density and hair will be de-volumised in random slices with Headlines Crème.

1 Les cheveux sont épais et abondants. On réduit leur volume en prenant des mèches au hasard et en utilisant la crème Headlines.

1 Das Haar ist sehr schwer und füllig Das Volumen soll mit Headlines Crème abgebaut werden.

1 El cabello es grueso en texture y densidad. El cabello será reduci do en volumen mediante secciones paralelas con Headlines Crème.

1 I capelli sono spessi e folti. Il loro volume viene ridotto prendendo ciocche a caso e usando la crema Headlines.

3 Starting at the nape, diagonal slices are taken working around the perimeter of the head.

3 En partant de la nuque, prendre des mèches diagonales et ensuite continuer autour du périmètre de la tête.

3 Es wird am Nacken angefangen und diagonale um dem kontourenbereich herumgearbeitet.

3 Comenzando por la nuca se cojen secciones diagonales paralelas continuandolo por todo elperimetro de la cabeza.

3 Si prendono ciocche diagonali partendo dalla nuca e proseguendo poi attorno al perimetro della testa.

52

Technique – Texturising Headlines
Hair prior: no previous chemical treatments.

Technique – Texturising Headlines
Cheveux avant la coloration: aucun traitement chimique précédent.

Tachnik – Texturising Headlines
Haare nicht chemisch behandelt.

Técnica – Texturising Headlines
Usando cabello que no tiene ningun trataniento de chinica.

Tecnica – Texturising Headlines
Capelli prima del trattamento: nessun trattamento chimico precedente.

2 The Slices are taken with Headlines Forming Crème for Normal hair, it is applied using colour wraps.

2 Prendre des mèches de cheveux et, en utilisant des papiers pour la couleur, mettre la crème Headlines Forming pour cheveux normaux.

2 Headlines Forming Crème für normales Haar wird auf scheibensträhnen mit Tigi Meche aufgetragen.

2 Se cojen particiones con Headlines Forming Crème para cabello normal utilizando papeles para el color.

2 Si prendono ciocche di capelli e, servendosi di cartine per il colore, si pone la crema Headlines Forming per capelli normali.

5 The result is multi-textured.

5 On obtient un résultat de différents volumes.

5 Das Ergebnis ist eine Mehrfach Textur.

5 El resultado es multi-texturado.

5 Si ottiene un risultato di diversi volumi.

53

4 The completed application. Directional slices are in the internal shape to achieve texture throughout. The hair is developed for 5–20mins depending on the degree of control required. Hair was then fixed with Headlines Fixative.

4 Après avoir terminé avec le périmètre de la tête, prendre des mèches de cheveux à l'intérieur du cercle, ainsi qu'on obtienne un effet uniforme dans toute la tête. Le temps de pose varie entre 5 et 20 minutes, selon le degré de contrôle qu'on veut obtenir. Ensuite les cheveux sont fixés avec Headlines Fixative.

4 Nach dem Auftragen Scheibensträhnen werden diagonale genommen um dem Haar Textur zu geben. Die Einwirkzeit beträgt 5–20 minuten und ist abhängig daron wieriel volumen abgebaut werden soll. Das Haar wird dann mit Headlines Fixative fixiert.

4 Completada la aplicacion, secciones paralelas, en la zona interna para conseguir textura por todo el cabello.

4 Una volta completato il perimetro della testa, si procede prendendo ciocche di capelli nella parte interna a questo cerchio, in modo da ottenere un effetto uniforme in tutta la testa. I capelli vengono poi lasciati in posa per 5–20 minuti, in base al grado di controllo che si vuole ottenere. In seguito viene posto il fissatore Headlines Fixative.

2 Pivot around the crown area pulling the hair out at 90° from the back of the head. Then the hair is slice cut.

2 Pivoter autour du point d'éclatement en lissant les cheveux à 90 degrés à l'arrière de la tête. Couper une ligne recte avec les ciseaux à la verticale.

2 Mit dem wirvelals Drepunkt wird das Haar im 90° Winkelrausgezogen und eine gerade linie mit "point-cutting" – Technik geschnitten.

2 Estirar el pelo a 90' de la zona de atras de la cabeza. Cortar a punta de tijera una linea recta.

2 Si prendono sezioni di capelli nella parte posteriore della testa, facendo perno nella zona della corona. I capelli vengono portati fuori a 90 gradi e si taglia una linea retta usando la tecnica del "point cut".

1 The centre parting is to the crown area. Then work horizontal sections to the high point of the ear.

1 Tracer une raie centrale jusqu áu point d'éclatement. Ensuite travailler en sections horizontales jusqu'à la pointe des oreilles.

1 Mittelscheitel bis zum wirbel. Dann werden horizontale Abteilungen zum höchsten punkt des Ohres gezogen.

1 Partición central hasta la zona de la coronilla. Trabajar sección horizontal hasta el punto alto de la oreja.

1 Si traccia una linea centrale fino alla calotta. In seguito si lavora in sezioni orizzontali fino alla punta delle orecchie.

3 Follow the guide from the back, through to the sides using vertical sections, slicing the hair.

3 Suivre le guide de l'arrière en avançant vers le côté et faire des sections verticales. Couper en ligne recte avec les ciseaux à la verticale.

3 Die hintere Fürungslinie wird zu den seiten verfolgt. Es werden vertikale Abteilungen gezogen. (Point-cutting-technik.)

3 Sequir la guia desde atrás los lados utilizando secciones verticales.

3 Usando come guida la parte posteriore, si prosegue lungo i lati della testa, tracciando sezioni verticali. Si taglia nuovamente una linea retta con la tecnica del "point cut".

4 Pull the hair up at 90° from the top of the head using horizontal sections and slice cut a square line.

4 Prendre des section horizontales dans la partie haute de la tête et lisser les cheveux à 90 degrés. Couper une ligne recte.

4 Das Haar wird im 90° – Winkel vom oberkopf vausgezogen und mit horizontalen Abteilungen zu einer geraden Linie geschnitten.

4 Estirar el cabello a 90° de la parte superior la cabeza utilizando secciones horizontales y cortar una linea recta.

4 Si prendono sezioni orizzontali nella parte alta della testa, si portano i capelli verso l'alto a 90 gradi e si taglia una linea retta.

5 Personalise to suit.

5 Personaliser selon le goût.

5 Der Haarschnitt wird typgerecht personalisiert.

5 Personalizar el corte.

5 Il taglio viene personalizzato in modo adeguato.

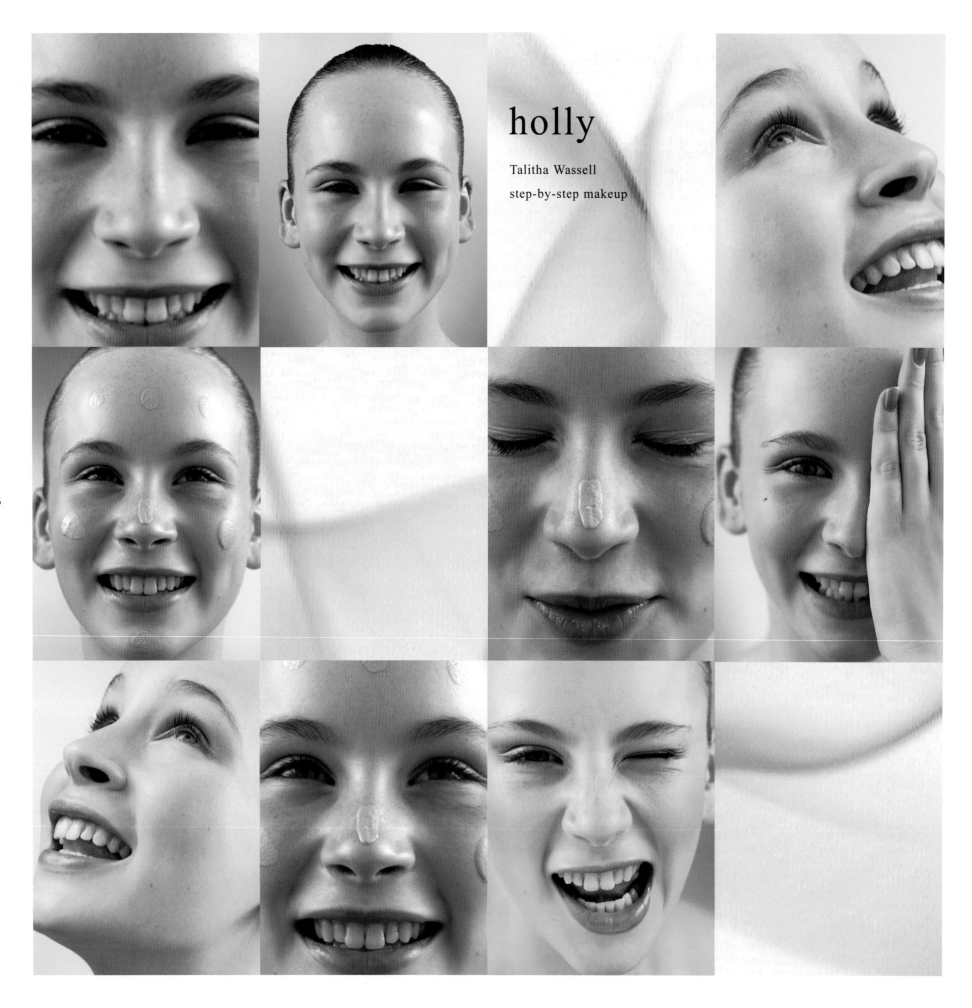

holly

Talitha Wassell

step-by-step makeup

56

2 Apply a small amount of foundation (porcelain) to the jawbone to ensure the colour is suitable for skin tone. Blend foundation using small downward strokes, starting from the centre, blending outwards. Use a sponge for even application.

2 Mettre une petite quantité de fond de teint (porcelaine) sur le maxillaire pour s'assurer que la couleur est adéquate à la couleur de la peau. Mélanger le fond de teint avec des petites touches de main, en commençant du centre et en descendant vers le bas. On peut utiliser une éponge pour une application plus uniforme.

2 Es wird eine passende Grundierung (Porcelain) auf den Kinnknochen aufgtragen. Die Grundierung wird durch kleine Wischbewegungen nach unten eigeblendet. Esd wird vonm der Mitte aus angefangen und nach aussenhitgearbeitet. Fuer eine gleichmaessige Auftragung dient ein Schwaemmonen.

2 Para asegurarse de que la base combine con el color de piel, aplique una prueba en la mandíbula. Una vez que elija el color, aplique una cantidad en distintos puntos de la cara y con una esponja de maquillaje expanda la base en dirección al cuello.

2 Porre una piccola quantita' di fondotinta (porcellana) sulla mandibola, per accertarsi che il colore sia adatto al colore della pella. Spalmare il fondotinta con piccoli tocchetti di mano partendo dal centro e scendendo verso il basso. Si puo' usare una spugnetta per un'applicazione piu' uniforme.

58

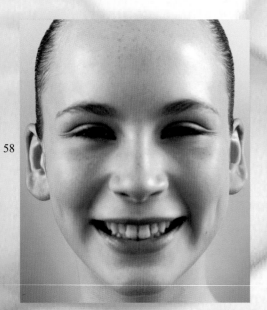

1 Cleanse, tone and moisturise the face and neck (essential preparation).

1 Nettoyer, tonifier et hydrater le visage, le cou (préparation essentielle).

1 Das Gesicht wird gereinigt, Gesichtswasser und Feuchtigkeitscreme werden aufgetragen.

1 Empezar con una leche limpiadora, aplicar después un tónico astringente y terminar con una crema de cutis.

1 Pulire, tonificare e idratare il viso e il collo (preparazione essenziale).

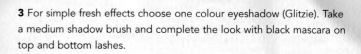

3 For simple fresh effects choose one colour eyeshadow (Glitzie). Take a medium shadow brush and complete the look with black mascara on top and bottom lashes.

3 Pour un effet simple et frais, choisir une seule couleur d'ombre à paupières (Glitzie); utiliser une brosse moyenne. Pour completer le look, mettre du mascara noir sur les cils d'en haut et d'en bas.

3 Fuer einen natuerlichen frishen Effekt wird ein Colour Eyeshadow (Glitzie) gewaehlt und mit einem mittldicken Pinsel aufgetragen. Um de Look vollstaendig zu machen wird Schwarze Mascara auf die oberen und unteren Wimpern aufgetragen.

3 Para un efecto fresco y natural elija un solo color de sombra brillante y use un aplicador de sombra mediano. Termine el efecto con las pestañas usando una máscara negra.

3 Per un effetto semplice e fresco, scegliere un solo colore di ombretto (Glitzie); usare un pennello medio. Completare il look usando mascara di colore nero sulle ciglia in alto e in basso.

4 Apply a light covering of blusher (latte) to the apple of the cheek using a large blusher brush for a healthy glow.

4 Mettre un voil de fard à joues (latte) sur les joues en utilisant une grosse brosse pour un effet naturel.

4 Ein Hauch Rouge (latte) wird auf den oberen Teil der Wenge mit einem dicken Pinsel aufgetragen um einen gesunden Gesichtston zu kreieren.

4 Aplique una cantidad mínima de color en la parte central de la mejilla. Use un aplicador de colorete grande para terminar el efecto con naturalidad y brillo.

4 Porre un velo leggero di fard (latte) sulle guance, usando un pennello grande per un effetto naturale.

6 To complete the look, apply a light coloured (Champagne) lipstick. Avoid using lipliner to keep the look natural. To finish apply a slick of lip-gloss for a touch of glamour!

6 Pour completer le look, utiliser un rouge à lèvres de couleur claire (Champagne). Eviter d'utiliser le crayon à lèvres, pour garder un effet naturel. Pour donner une touche d'éclat, mettre un petit peu de brilliant transparent.

6 Um den Look zu vervollstaendigen wird ein heller Lipperstift (champagne) aufgetragen. Auf Lipliner wird verzichtet um das Make up natuerlicher aussehen zu lassen. Am Schluss wird noch etwas Lipgloss aufgetragen, dies, aesst das Make up etwas glamouroeser aussehen.

6 Para terminar el efecto, aplique solo una pintura de labios color champagne. No use delineador de labios para mantener el efecto natural. Para el toque final, aplique un poco de brillo de labios.

6 Per completare il look, usare un rossetto di colore chiaro (Champagne), evitando la matita per le labbra, in modo da mantenere un look naturale. Per finire, dare un tocco di fascino usando una goccia di lucidalabbra.

59

5 Using a reflective eyeshadow (Glitzie) apply a small amount to the temple area, blending down to top of cheekbone. This creates the effect of high cheekbones.

5 Mettre une petite quantité d'ombre à paupières brilliant sur la zone des tempes et descendre vers la pommette. De cette façon la pommette est mise en évidence.

5 Nun wird Eyeshadow (Glitzie) auf die Schlaefen aufgetragen und zum oberen Wangenknochen eingeblendet. Dies kreiret den Effekt eines hoeheren Wangenknochen.

5 Usando una sombra con brillo, aplique una mínima cantidad en la área de las sienes difuminándola hacia la parte superior de la mejilla.

5 Porre una piccola quantita' di ombretto lucido (Glitzie) sulle zona delle tempie, sfumando in basso verso gli zigomi. In questo modo si fa sembrare che gli zigomi siano alti.

Products used: Liquid Foundation with vitamin E in porcelain. Duo eyeshadow in Glitzie. Mascara in Black. Lipstick in Champagne. Lip-gloss in Clear

Produits utilises: Fond de teint liquide avec vitamine E – porcelaine. Ombre à paupière Duo – Glitzie. Rouge à lèvres – Champagne. Brilliant – Transparent

Verwandete Produkte: Liquid Foundation mit Vitamin E Porcelin. Duo Eyeshadow Glitzie. Mascara Black. Lipstick Champagne. Lipgloss Clear

Productos: base líquida con vitamina E – Porcelain. Sombra – Glitzie. Máscara – negra. Pintura de labios – Champagne. Brillo de labios – transparente.

Prodotti usati: Fondotinta liquido con vitamina E – porcellana. Ombretto Duo – Glitzie. Mascara – Nero. Rossetto – Champagne. Lucidalabbra – Trasparente.

Founded in 1997 by Toni Mascolo, Chairman of TONI&GUY, Essensuals represents a new generation of hairdressing for Century 21 and was created to fill a gap in the hairdressing market for high quality hairdressing at a competitive price.

The Mission:

To create quality hairstyling at affordable prices for contemporary men and women.

The Concept:

Essensuals is the diffusion line of the TONI&GUY salon group, using all the resources and experience of it's mother company, yet maintaining and promoting it's own image and identity.

The Philosophy:

To provide a lifestyle approach for their client's well being and image by incorporating hair, beauty and makeup all under one roof. .

Success Breeds Success

Everybody wants a piece of Essensuals, do you?

Why would so many hairdressers choose to open an Essensuals franchise rather than opening an independent salon? The answer is simple Success Breeds Success

The Essensuals franchise program has been devised from experience gained over 35 years in the hair-dressing market and over 12 years experience of running an international franchise operation.

Essensuals franchisees receive complete support from the outset. The company's financial status helps to obtain prime premises and bank loans. From the business plan, salon interior design and shop fitting to accounts procedures all the pain is taken out of setting up and running your business.

Education and Training

Dedication to outstanding hairdressing means that all Essensuals staff must commit to ongoing training provided by the company academy. The educational program based on the world renowned Toni&Guy system ensures that quality is maintained across the group and gives franchisees extra pulling power for recruiting and maintaining staff. Devised by Educational Director, Christian Mascolo, all Essensuals staff are trained to be strong and confident with both cutting and technical work. The training however is not just about hairdressing, staff are also taught to work as part of a team, to have awareness and consideration of fashion trends plus learning the importance of client care and service.

Image and PR

Essensuals has been founded with the benefit of many years of experience in creating commercially appealing images and a strong PR message. The fresh approach that Sacha and Christian Mascolo have brought to Essensuals takes the company to a new level of imagery that is both young at heart, totally wearable and widely appealing. Sacha Mascolo, Creative Director is responsible for the group's image. As the daughter of Toni Mascolo, Sacha was literally born into hairdressing and from an early age showed natural talent for it. Sacha still works closely with her uncle Anthony Mascolo – 3 times British Hairdresser of the year, as Show Director for Toni&Guy, however more and more of her time is now being dedicated to Essensuals as the young company continues to grow from strength to strength.

1999 saw Sacha win the coveted 'London Hairdresser' title at the annual British Hairdressing Awards. Now in August 2000, Sacha has made it through to the final stage again in the London category and has also been nominated for the Session Hairdresser category.

Recently Sacha has been working with David Bailey as a session stylist on a number of high profile magazines such as Harpers & Queen, Scene, Sky, Tatler and Vogue. The value of advertising locally, nationally and internationally is never underestimated and a large budget is assigned for this purpose annually. An ongoing campaign in women's consumer press ensures that the corporate brand is promoted to the chosen target audience.

Essensuals Services
Hair, Beauty, Make up, Bridal

The combination of all of the above services is important to offer clients the lifestyle approach that Essensuals represents.

All hair products used and retailed in Essensuals salons are made by TIGI Haircare, a professional range of products developed by TONI&GUY. The group's size ensures that every franchisee receives substantial discounts on all in salon products. TIGI also provide all cosmetic products, this relatively new line in make-up is proving a success and boosts retail sales considerably.

Essensuals Suppliers and Associated Businesses

Several companies have been created in the past few years as the rate of expansion across the group has snowballed to the point that is became necessary to form specialised companies solely working within the Mascolo Group.

Straight impact – Project management and Shop-fitters.

Innovia Design – takes care of all your salon requirements from furniture to stationery, to cups and saucers, coffee machines and TIGI products.

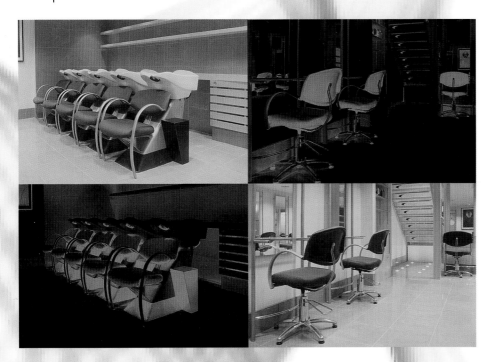

SALONGENIUS Mascolo Support Systems – suppliers of Salon Genius – a computerised salon management, till and marketing package designed by hairdressers to be used by hairdressers. Mascolo Support provides hardware and software together with full training and internet support.

With all this support from the Mascolo group plus the client confidence and trust that is brought about by the strong brand name, opening and running a successful business has never been easier. For any further information on franchising please contact Clarissa Martin in the Franchise Department on: T: 020 8844 0008 or clarissa@mascolo.co.uk, alternatively contact Alex on T: 020 7440 6690 or alex@essensuals.co.uk.